CAFFEINE + CONFUSION

Steven Case

THE PILGRIM PRESS
Cleveland

This book is dedicated to the youth of the
Windermere Union Church, United Church of Christ.
They are, without a doubt, the finest group of young people that
I have ever worked with. It is my honor to be called
their minister.

The Pilgrim Press, 700 Prospect Avenue, Cleveland, Ohio 44115-1100
thepilgrimpress.com
© 2008 by Steven Case

Scripture quotations, unless otherwise noted, are from the New
Revised Standard Version of the Bible, © 1989 by the Division of
Christian Education of the National Council of Churches of Christ in
the United States of America and are used by permission. Changes
have been made for inclusivity.

13 12 11 10 09 08   5 4 3 2 1

Library of Congress Cataloging-in-Publication Data

Case, Steve L., 1964-
  Caffeine and confusion / Steven Case.
    p. cm.
  ISBN 978-0-8298-1809-3 (alk. paper)
  1. Youth--Religious life. 2. Devotional exercises. I. Title.
  BV4531.3.C3677 2008
  242'.63--dc22
                                2008014440

CONTENTS

MAN OVERBOARD!

THEME: SALVATION

ORDER HERE

In the Old Testament the word "salvation" is from the Hebrew *y shuw'ah* (yesh-ooo-aw), which means "deliverance" (as in the people of Israel). In the New Testament the word was the Greek *soteria* (so-tay-ree-ah), which means something more like "rescue." Salvation has come to be one of those litmus tests of faith: Are you saved (or not)? There may be conditions on discipleship, but there are none on salvation. The Bible says, "Turn to me and be saved." Face me. Look at me. It doesn't say complete this form or repeat this prayer. Just, "Look at me."

START THINKING

True or False?

- Cooking is about following the recipe to the ¼ tsp., with no variation.
- The greatest meals come only after a dozen burned ones.
- If someone gives me a new gadget as a gift, I'll spend hours poring over the instructions before turning it on.
- I have, on more than one occasion, fried a gadget or computer because I

didn't put it together correctly.

- From the ashes of disaster grow the roses of success.
- A stained cookbook means love.
- If your Bible is falling apart, chances are you are not.
- Everyone is born a sinner.
- Every good thing we do "down here" is another piece of lumber for our house in heaven.
- When it comes right down to it, the only people who will be in heaven are the ones who knowingly, of their own choice, accept Jesus Christ as their personal Lord and Savior.

TABLE NOTES

A horn, a helmet, a shield, a lamp, a cup, clothing, a tower, a chariot: all of these words are used in the scriptures to describe salvation. Based on what you know or have been told, draw a picture of salvation.

SCRIPTURE MENU

Have someone read the verses and another ask the questions aloud.

Psalm 103:11-12 (TNCH)

For as the heavens are high above the earth,
  so great is God's steadfast love toward those
    who fear God;
as far as the east is from the west,
  so far God removes our transgressions
    from us.

Have you ever tried to lug too much baggage through an airport? How is this an image of how some people think of approaching God?

Isaiah 45:22 (NRSV)

Turn to me and be saved, all the ends of the earth! For I am God, and there is no other.

This is the "turn to me verse." Think of five things that this verse does not say are requirements for being "saved." (Examples: wearing particularly "cool" clothes; memorizing scripture.) Don't make this question harder than it is.

Romans 14:7 (NRSV)

We do not live to ourselves, and we do not die to ourselves.

Why do you suppose some people who are officially "saved" believe it is their responsibility to save others? Do we have a responsibility to do just that? If we do not "live" to ourselves and we do not "die" to ourselves, how do we acknowledge that connection to all things?

In your opinion, is the process of faith more like fuzzy slippers or a pair of pants that are too small? Make your own analogy.

Isaiah 25:6 (NIV)

On this mountain the Lord Almighty will prepare
  a feast of rich food for all peoples,
a banquet of aged wine—
  the best of meats and the finest of wines.

Salvation comes from God and "all peoples" get it. If everyone is saved and no one is excluded from God's table...what's the point of living a good life? Why can't we just be nasty and cheat and lie to each other? Oswald Chambers said, "My life is my way of saying 'thank you.'" How does your church say "thank you" to God? How do you say "thank you" in your own life?

2 Peter 1:5 (NRSV)
For this very reason, you must make every effort to support your faith with goodness, and goodness with knowledge...

Look at this verse. Choose something (an event or an action) that you think symbolizes faith. How do you add goodness to that? What is the result? Now add knowledge. What's the end result?

Choose something you do every day. Add goodness and knowledge to it. What do you get?

TAKE HOME BAG

In the space below, write down three words—Yesterday, Today, Tomorrow.

Circle the word that seems to give you the most trouble.

TIP

You know how you feel the week before a concert for which you have tickets? That's how God wants you to feel all the time.

MY BOOK IS BREATHING!

THEME: BIBLE

ORDER HERE

The Bible is a collection of stories and, at the same time, one continuous story that began before the book begins and continues long after the last chapter concludes. It is the account of God's dealings with creation and God's hopes for our continued growth. It is a coloring book without lines. It is poetry and promises. It is not a textbook or a history book, and, above all else, it is not finished.

START THINKING

True or False?

- When I get a new gadget or gizmo, I study the instruction manual from cover to cover. Then I turn it on.
- The ingredients list in a recipe is just a guideline.
- When I go to a buffet restaurant, I mix all the different drinks into one cup.
- The Bible is a "take-it-or-leave-it" instruction book.
- The Bible was written by God through the hands of some very special people.
- The Bible is a history book that opens doors into the minds of those who lived in the time it was written.

- The Bible is so full of contradictions that it's really impossible to take it seriously.
- The Bible is a violent barrier-building book that has caused way more problems than it has solved.
- There are no easy answers.

TABLE NOTES

Do you have a pet? If you don't, imagine that you do. Make a list of things that your pet needs from you and a list of what your pet provides for you.

What would happen if we looked at the Bible as a living and breathing presence in our lives? How can you take some of the items in your lists about your pet and apply them to a "relationship" with the Bible?

SCRIPTURE MENU

Have someone look up the verses, and ask the questions aloud.

Read Psalm 119:97–106.

What do you expect from the Bible?

Which of these objects most closely fits how you currently see the Bible?

Rock   Scissors   Paper   Honey   Lamp   Window   Mirror

Explain your answer. If none of these quite fits, come up with your own object to compare the Bible to.

Is the Bible sacred or is it the message that's sacred? (Or both? Or neither?)

Is it okay to write in the Bible?

Some believe that if your Bible is falling apart, chances are you are not. What does this mean? Do you think it's true?

In the movie *Saved*, one girl literally throws the Bible at a fellow student. The student picks it up and responds, "This is not a weapon, you idiot." How is the Bible used (perhaps not quite so literally) as a weapon?

Read 2 Timothy 3:14–17 (NRSV).

This passage says the Bible is inspired. It also says the Bible is useful for:

Teaching
Rebuking
Correcting
Training
Equipping for good works

How have you used or how has the Bible been used like each of these in your life?

Psalm 119:18–20 (NIV)
¹⁸**Open my eyes that I may see**
   wonderful things in your law.
¹⁹**I am a stranger on earth;**
   do not hide your commands from me.
²⁰**My soul is consumed with longing**
   for your laws at all times.

Read 2 Chronicles 34:1–18.

Imagine if you sold everything you own, wandered the earth for years borrowing money and receiving donations of money, and finally used all that you had saved and bought the hottest car on the planet. On your first drive, before you even started the engine, you opened the glove compartment and found a copy of the Bible. How would you feel?

Every one of these verses talks about the Bible's inspiration:

Exodus 20:1; 24:4, 24:12, 25:2, 31:18, 32:16, 34:27, 34:32	Psalms 78:5, 99:7, 147:19
Leviticus 26:46	Eccles. 12:11
Deuteronomy 4:5, 4:14, 11:18, 31:19, 31:22	Isaiah 30:12-13, 34:16, 59:21
2 Kings 17:13	Jeremiah 30:2, 36:1-2, 36:27-28, 36:32, 51:5-64
2 Chronicles 33:18	Ezekiel 11:25
Job 23:12	Daniel 10:21
	Hosea 8:12

Zechariah 7:12	1 Timothy 6:3-5
Matthew 22:31-32;	2 Timothy 3:16-17
Luke 1:1-4, 1:68-73	Hebrews 1:1-2, 3:7-8, 4:12, 5:12
Acts 1:16, 28:25	1 Peter 1:11-12
Romans 3:1-2	2 Peter 1:21, 3:2, 3:15
1 Corinthians 2:12-13, 7:10, 14:37	1 John 1:1-5
Ephesians 6:17	Revelation 1:1-2, 1:11, 1:17-19, 2:7,
Colossians 3:16	19:10, 22:6-8
1 Thessalonians 2:131, 4:1-3	

"Inspiration" comes from the Latin word *inspiratus*, which means "spirit or breath." It also means "to inflame, to influence, to blow into, to animate."

When are you at your creative best?

There is a tradition in the Jewish faith that if you come across a passage or phrase that sounds like something else you have read, you must go back and find that first phrase and see how the two (or three or four or one hundred) are similar to each other. What would happen if WE read the Bible this way?

Off the top of your head, can you think of any Bible passages that are "similar"?

What if the Bible is God's way of breathing?

TAKE HOME BAG

Read Exodus 20:1 (the first verse from the inspiration list).
Use that verse as a prayer the next time you open the Bible to read.

How to read the Bible:

1. Pray

2. Read out loud.

3. Pay attention to word or phrases that "jump" out at you.

4. Think about who this was written for, who heard it first, who will hear it later.

5. Ask yourself, How can I make this phrase/word/passage breathe?

KNOCK, KNOCK, KNOCKIN'

THEME: WHAT IS HEAVEN?

ORDER HERE

What if you died and woke up to find that heaven was exactly like you were taught in Sunday school—everybody sitting on clouds, little naked angles floating around playing harps...In the words of Steve Martin, "Wouldn't you feel stupid?"

Heaven is different things to different people, but the Bible does tell us that we don't really have a clue about it. Imagine all your senses as being limitations. What happens when we no longer need those? What if we have a thousand senses in heaven? We "know" that heaven is a "place" or a realm so far beyond our "knowing" that Disney's best creative team couldn't come close to imagining what God has in store for us. So let's take a look at the things we do know.

START THINKING

True or False?

- In heaven I get my pets back.
- Saint Peter is sitting at a big desk with a big book ready to check off my

name if I've been good enough.

- I've been good enough.
- In heaven I will get my own wings and halo.
- In heaven there is no beer.

TABLE NOTES

The writer Kurt Vonnegut created a heaven where people could peer down a well and see what was going on in hell. Writer Robert Heinlein created a vision of heaven in his book Job *that looked like an out-of-control Macy's Parade. Draw a picture of what you think heaven looks like.*

SCRIPTURE MENU

Read or look up one or more of the passages, and respond to the discussion suggestions that follow.

1 Corinthians 2:9 (NIV)
However, as it is written:
 "No eye has seen,
  no ear has heard,
 no mind has conceived
  what God has prepared for those
   who love him."

Read Isaiah 65:17–25.

The prophet (God speaking through a person) gives us a description of "heaven." What does this description say about the people it was being written for? What was their life like?

Joel 3:17–21 (NRSV)

¹⁷So you shall know that I, the Lord your God,
   dwell in Zion, my holy mountain.
And Jerusalem shall be holy,
   and strangers shall never again
      pass through it.

¹⁸In that day
the mountains shall drip sweet wine,
   the hills shall flow with milk,
and all the stream beds of Judah shall flow with water;
a fountain shall come forth from
      the house of the Lord and water the Wadi Shittim.

¹⁹Egypt shall become a desolation
   and Edom a desolate wilderness,
because of the violence done to the
      people of Judah, in whose land they have shed
      innocent blood.
²⁰But Judah shall be inhabited
      forever, and Jerusalem to all generations.
²¹I will avenge their blood, and I will
      not clear the guilty,
   for the Lord dwells in Zion.

Read Amos 9:13–15.

None of the prophets talks about heaven as a place that we "go to" after we die.

Much of their writings were based on the idea of a barter economy, in which everybody had something and shared it with everybody else so that everybody had what they needed.

These two passages talk about heaven in terms of "restoration." What would happen if heaven is really earth "repaired"? How would you fix earth?

Imagine an earth that has none of the negatives that makes living here a bad thing. Imagine your life with no more "bad days." Is that hard to think about?

1 Corinthians 15:42-44 (MsgB)

⁴²This image of planting a dead seed and raising a live plant is a mere sketch at best, but perhaps it will help in approaching the mystery of the resurrection body—but only if you keep in mind

that when we're raised, we're raised for good, alive forever! **43**The corpse that's planted is no beauty, but when it's raised, it's glorious. Put in the ground weak, it comes up powerful. **44**The seed sown is natural; the seed grown is supernatural—same seed, same body, but what a difference from when it goes down in physical mortality to when it is raised up in spiritual immortality!

Paul doesn't talk about souls going to heaven. He talks about a "resurrection body" that reunites with the soul. If heaven and earth were in fact the same place, what would that look like?

Luke 13:29 (NIV)
People will come from east and west and north and south, and will take their places at the feast in the kingdom of God.

Who gets into heaven?

What does your denomination teach about heaven?

Why is it important to some people that not everybody gets into heaven?

Is it important to you for heaven to be "someplace else"? Why or why not?

Read Matthew 6:8.
Read the verse with new eyes. What if it's an invitation?

TAKE HOME BAG

If heaven on earth is a place where people take what they have and share it with people who don't have (but have something else) and everyone makes sure everyone else has what they need, what do you have that you can share this week?

TIP
It's going to get a lot better. Regardless of what else you believe, believe that.

A TERRIBLE GNASHING

THEME: WHAT IS HELL?

ORDER HERE

If we are going to ask some new questions about heaven, shouldn't we also ask questions about hell? For some people, hell becomes the reason to be saved. Not the reward of heaven but the complete and total fear of going to a place of eternal damnation. Fear becomes the motivator for behavior. A child does not write on the walls because of a fear that daddy will give the child a swat on the bum. People who are afraid of hell don't see the love behind the father. The concept of forgiveness becomes foreign, and all the things we think are unclean or unsightly get buried deep down in our souls until we create a hell right here on earth. Nobody wants to go there.

Like a discussion of heaven, the subject of hell stirs deep feelings in some people and opinions are held very close. Our purpose here is not so much to find answers as to embrace questions.

START THINKING

Choose one.

- I would rather burn in the everlasting lake of lava / meet a purple cow.
- I am most afraid of spiders / snakes/ the dark / squishy things.
- I am most effective when I am under pressure / inspired.
- I would rather ride in an inner tube on a calm lake in summer / surf in a storm.
- I will vote for the person who will do the most good / I will vote for the person who will do *me* the most good.
- The devil made me do it. / I made a stupid choice.

True or False?

- I have listened to (watched, read, played) a certain (disc, book, band) simply because I was told it was evil, and I'll be dammed for doing it.

TABLE NOTES

Draw a picture of "classic" TV and movie hell.

SCRIPTURE MENU

The word "hell" does not occur in the Old Testament. You may find the Greek work *Hades* or the Hebrew word *Sheol*, which were both words for the same thing. They were used to describe a "place of the dead" or "place for disembodied souls." Jesus refers to hell eight times—twelve if you count the places where the Gospels repeat one another.

SHEOL, HADES, AND GEHENNA

"Sheol" comes from a word meaning "to ask" or "to demand." It implies an insatiableness, or the inability to be satisfied. Sheol is a dark place or, more accurately, a place that is "unseen." The word is used in the Old Testament thirty-one times.

"Hades" refers to a "place of the dead." It is where both good and bad souls go to await judgment.

Now we'll look at the word "Gehenna" as Jesus used it.

Read these verses:

Matthew 5:22, 29-30; 10:28; 18:9; 23:15, 33
Luke 16:23
James 2:6

Jesus was talking to:

people who objectify others.

people who are hypocrites.

people who put themselves between God and others.

people who put their respect in the wrong places.

Gehenna was not a hidden mystical place but an actual area near Jerusalem that was used as a sort of garbage dump for all sorts of trash, dead animals, and the bodies of dead prisoners. A fire was kept burning there all the time to dispose of the trash. The area was also the place where packs of wild dogs would roam to find stuff to eat.

Jesus never said that Gehenna was a "final destination." It was a very present "now" word. Jesus used it as an analogy to describe the hearts and minds of religious leaders of the time. What's an example of hell as a "present condition" today?

"Racca" is a term of contempt. It means someone is about to hock up a lugie on you. If a place where people have no respect for one another is a "hell on earth," where is an example of that today? Is there a place in your life where there is "hell?"

What happens when we spend all our time worrying about all the stupid things in our lives? Aren't we essentially creating a hell on earth?

Jesus is talking to the disciples and to the religious leaders of the day. If he were here today, who would Jesus be talking to?

Where are the "hells" on earth today and how can we bring "heaven" to them?

Who do you know who is "living in hell"? (No names out loud.) What can you do to bring that person some heaven?

Take Home Bag

Take some time this week to watch the news. If hell is an "attitude" or a "way of living" and not a physical place, how many "hells" do you see in a thirty-minute newscast? How many are of a person's own creation?

Now ask yourself honestly: Have you ever created "hell on earth" for someone else?

Tip

"Travel has no longer any charm for me. I have seen all the foreign countries I want to except heaven & hell & I have only a vague curiosity about one of those."

—Mark Twain, in a letter to W. D. Howells, 1891

WHERE THE HELL HAVE YOU BEEN?

Theme: SATAN

ORDER HERE

There is no image of the red-skinned guy with horns and a pitchfork in the Bible. Yet people hold this image as close to them as they do the classic image of Jesus. The question is, Do you believe in Satan the devil, the tempter, as an actual being who is responsible for the thorn on the rose and the stinger on the bee? Or to you, does the word "satan" (note small "s") refer to anything that gets into God's path for God's people? Are the stories about the devil in the Bible literally true, or did the writers need a "personification" of evil to get people to pay attention?

START THINKING

Choose one.

- *The Devil Wears Prada* / *The Exorcist*
- "Black & White" / *Shades of Gray*
- Memorize the instruction book. / There's an instruction book?
- God made the bee, and Satan made the stinger. / God made both for a reason.

- God will let me get an F to teach me something. / Satan made me get an F. / I probably should have studied.
- Some people claim there's a woman to blame, but I know it's nobody's fault. / Hell—it could be my fault. / It's my own damn fault.

TABLE NOTES

What's the greatest portrayal of the devil in any movie or TV show you've ever seen? Draw a picture of a classic devil.

SCRIPTURE MENU

There are many passages in the Bible that refer to an embodied evil. Some say the snake in the Garden of Eden was Satan. Others point to the image of the dragon in John's Revelation. We're going to look at just a few of these scriptures. First, though, some history:

- In Christian writings the word "satan" means adversary or accuser.
- In the New Testament, the words "Satan" and "Devil" are interchangeable.

Read Genesis 3:1–13.

Lucifer, the name given to Satan, means "bright star" or "bringer of light," and Lucifer is referred to a few times in the Old Testament. How does the idea of "bringer of light" fit into the stories we know about Lucifer?

Have you ever heard the phrase "the Devil made me do it"? What does it mean?

Do you believe that evil is something that can go in and out of you, or do we all have the capacity for great good and great evil within us?

Much of your belief in a "devil" may come from your personal beliefs about the scriptures. Do you believe in a literal translation of the Bible? All of it or just parts of it? What were you taught as a child about the devil?

Read Job 1:6–12.

Here Satan just seems to show up in heaven. Various translations have God saying everything from "Whence comest thou?" (KJV) to "What have you been up to?" (Msg). Either way, God does not seem all that upset to see a formerly favorite angel return. In the book of Job, it is God and not Satan who turns Job's life into a shambles for what seems to be a wager between God and Satan.

Do you think God would mess with your life just to see how you react? Have you ever (metaphorically) shaken a fist at the heavens and said, "Why God? Why?"

Read Isaiah 14:12–15.

Matthew 16:23 (NIV)
But he turned and said to Peter, "Get behind me, Satan! You are a stumbling block to me; for you are setting your mind not on divine things but on human things."

Why would Jesus call Peter the name Satan? If we take a different translation, or perhaps a more literal one, Jesus says, "Don't tempt me."

The French poet Charles Baudelaire is credited with the phrase, "The greatest trick the devil ever pulled off was convincing the world that he didn't exist." Do you think this is true?

Does Christianity work without a villain?

What if our thinking about Satan has been muddled by time and culture and the authors of the scriptures wanted to have a "face" to put on evil?

Do you believe in the satan or Satan? Part of the problem with believing the small "s" is that we have to take responsibility for our own actions. How well do we do that?

Could Satan exist without God's permission? Why would God allow Satan to exist in that form?

When we think of the personified Satan, isn't it usually as a being who is equal to God? It's an image that implies the "light and dark" and the "hero and villain," but isn't that the opposite of believing in one God?

TAKE HOME BAG

When you get home, read Romans 8:35–39. How does this passage apply to a discussion of Satan? Rewrite this passage in your own words and bring it to the next session.

TIP

"But who prays for Satan? Who in eighteen centuries has had the common humanity to pray for the one sinner that needed it most?"

—*Mark Twain*, in *The Autobiography of Mark Twain*

A GOOD JEWISH BOY

THEME: WHAT IS JUDAISM?

There is no way a few short pages of explorations can even come close to encompassing all the rich history and spiritual beauty of Judaism and Islam. It's just not possible. Our goal in this and the next Exploration is to provide a little context for our own faith. We hope to inspire thought and spark discussion.

ORDER HERE

Judaism is the world's oldest monotheistic faith—a faith that worships one God. Judaism, which has ties to both Christianity and Islam, is an on-going story of God's Covenant with Abraham and his descendants. Judaism is a continuing dialogue between God and God's chosen people. If they behave and believe, God will continue to sustain them throughout the generations.

START THINKING

Choose one.

● Some things just ARE: accept that without discussion. / Everything is debatable.

- God is good all the time. / All the time, God is good.
- Rules are rules. / Some rules are more important that others.
- I want to hear a story my grandmother learned from her grandmother. / Not right now, I'm blogging.
- God is here and knows which of these I will be choosing. / God is busy with more important things.
- I window shop on eBay. / Shopping is like hunting: get what you need and get out.
- The life of a killer is just as sacred as the life of the victim. / There's a reason we have capital punishment in this country.

TABLE NOTES

Imagine you are going to get a tattoo—simple yet detailed, abstract yet meaningful. Imagine that this tattoo will also be given to your children and to their children. A hundred generations from now, this tattoo will still be on the skin of all your descendants. It is to cement a promise between you and God that you will always have a relationship—whether that's one of anger fear, dancing, chatting, laughter...whatever. There will always be some kind of relationship there. Draw that tattoo here.

SCRIPTURE MENU

Read or look up one or more of the verses, and respond to the discussion suggestions that follow.

Genesis 12:1-3 (NIV)
¹The Lord had said to Abram, "Leave your country, your people and your

father's household and go to the land I will show you.

> ²"I will make you into a great nation
>   and I will bless you;
> I will make your name great,
>   and you will be a blessing.
> ³I will bless those who bless you,
>   and whoever curses you I will curse;
> and all peoples on earth
>   will be blessed through you."

What would you do if God showed you the night sky and said, "This is the number of your descendents. Do what I say. Go where I send you, and I will take care you of you forever"?

What would it take for you to actually believe God was speaking to you?

What would your first response be if God actually spoke to you?

Have you ever thought about your family line a thousand years from now? Describe what you envision.

What is the oldest story you know from your family tree? Do you think it will be told to your great great great great great great great great great great grandchildren?

THE TEN COMMANDMENTS
The Ten Commandments are essential to the Jewish faith and to Christianity. While Moses does appear in the Qur'an (the Islamic holy book), there is not a lot of support for the Commandments in Islamic writing.

Read Exodus 20:2–17.

In total there were 613 commands handed down by God. Early Jewish leaders believed all of these should be followed but that some were "lighter" (not as important as others) and some were "heavier" (extremely important). Look at the "Top Ten" and decided which ones you think are "heavier" and "lighter." Why do you think this?

BELIEFS FROM JUDAISM
These are some important beliefs in Judaism:

● All life is sacred.
● The soul goes on forever.

- The true nature of what the "soul" really is and what happens after we die are pretty much beyond our comprehension, so any thoughts on that should be left to God.
- The act of studying the Torah (the first five books of the Old Testament) is the same thing as praying.
- To say that faith is "group work" is putting it mildly.

JEWISH CEREMONIES

These are important Jewish ceremonies:

- Life itself—celebrate with strict adherence to tradition
- Rosh Hashanah—the Jewish New Year
- Yom Kippur—the Day of Atonement
- Chanukah—the Festival of Lights (*not* the "Jewish Christmas")
- Passover (Pesach)—celebrating the deliverance out of Egypt, when the angel of death "passed over" the houses of the Jewish slaves in Egypt

Take Home Bag

*On Yom Kippur (the Day of Atonement), the Jewish people believe they must ask God for forgiveness for bad things they did in the past year. But first they must go to the **people** they wronged and get their forgiveness. Are there things in your life you need to remedy before you go to God? Choose one of them and do one thing to fix that before the next session.*

Tip

"The Jews are a swinging bunch of people. I mean, I've heard of persecution, but what they have been through is just ridiculous. The great thing is that after thousands of years of waiting, and fighting, they finally made it."

—Sammy Davis Jr, as quoted by Bart Simpson,
in "Like Father Like Clown," "The Simpsons," season 1.

THE WORDS OF THE PROPHET

THEME: WHAT IS ISLAM?

ORDER HERE

The word "Islam" means "submission" (to God). It can also mean "peace." Many people believe that the prophet Muhammad was the creator or founder of Islam. This isn't true. Muhammad was the "last prophet" according to the Islamic faith. Like Judaism and Christianity, Islam has ties to the Old Testament.

START THINKING

Choose one.

- Praying is sitting in church with my hands folded / sitting with a bucket of sidewalk chalk by the side of a building.
- My most sacred place is the church sanctuary / Bethlehem / the ocean / the top of a mountain.
- The most sacred book ever written is the Bible / the Dead Sea Scrolls / the Book of Common Prayer / the dictionary.
- The religious practice that must look totally bizarre to people outside of our faith is the ritual of communion / funerals / weddings / full immersion baptism / vacation Bible school.

TABLE NOTES

Along with a belief in one God, angels, the words of the prophets, and a judgment day, Muslims also believe in "revealed" books—wisdom that already existed and was then "shown" to Muhammad.

Use your fanciest handwriting and write down a bit of wisdom that was given to you at some time in your life and still holds true.

SCRIPTURE MENU

Read or look up one or more of the verses, and respond to the discussion suggestions that follow.

Read Genesis 16:3, 15.
Read Genesis 21:10–14.

Many Muslims believe that when God promised to "make a great nation" of Ishmael, "the nation" God promised Abraham for his son Ishmael was the Nation of Islam. Ishmael and his mother settled in Mecca, the birthplace of Muhammad and the place of his revelation.

The Qur'an teaches that any representation of Muhammad or Allah (*the* God) is strictly forbidden. How many representations of Jesus or God do you have in your house? Why do you suppose the Christian faith has no problem with these?

Muhammad is "The Last Prophet," and it is to this prophet that God "revealed" the words that are the Qur'an. What does Christianity teach about those who wrote the Bible?

Read this passage from the Qur'an.

3. Al-'Imran 3.44–51

3.44**This is of the announcements relating to the unseen which We reveal to you; and you were not with them when they cast their pens (to decide) which of them should have Marium in his charge, and you were not with them when they contended one with another.**

3.45**When the angels said: "O Marium, surely Allah gives you good news with a Word from Him (of one) whose name is the Messiah, Isa, son of Marium, worthy of regard in this world and the hereafter and of those who are made near (to Allah).**

3.46**"And he shall speak to the people when in the cradle and when of old age, and (he shall be) one of the good ones."**

3.47**She said: "My Lord! When shall there be a son (born) to I me, and man has not touched me?" He said: "Even so, Allah creates what He pleases; when He has decreed a matter, He only says to it, 'Be,' and it is.**

3.48**"And He will teach him the Book and the wisdom and the Tavrat and the Injeel.**

3.49**"And (make him) an apostle to the children of Israel: 'That I have come to you with a sign from your Lord, that I determine for you out of dust like the form of a bird, then I breathe into it and it becomes a bird with Allah's permission and I heal the blind and the leprous, and bring the dead to life with Allah's permission and I inform you of what you should eat and what you should store in your houses; most surely there is a sign in this for you, if you are believers.**

3.50**'And a verifier of that which is before me of the Taurat and that I may allow you part of that which has been forbidden to you, and I have come to you with a sign from your Lord. Therefore be careful of (your duty to) Allah and obey me.**

3.51**'Surely Allah is my Lord and your Lord, therefore serve Him; this is the right path.'"**

This passage from the Qur'an sounds vaguely familiar, for Muslims recognize Jesus, though not as Messiah or divine. Jesus is one in a long line of prophets that ends with Muhammad. The Qur'an also refers to the angels Michael and Gabriel.

Does it seem odd to read the holy writings of another faith and see how they view Jesus? Explain.

There are five "Pillars," or obligations, that are required of those who claim the Muslim faith.

- Confession of Faith—"There is no God but Allah."
- Ritual Worship—praying five times a day
- Alms—offerings of treasure
- Fasting—during specific holy days
- Pilgrimage—Every Muslim is expected to make the journey to Mecca sometime in his or her life.

Are there "pillars" of Christianity? What are they?

TAKE HOME BAG

This first Surah (seven oft-repeated verses) is a prayer that is incorporated into all of Muslim worship:

1.1In the name of Allah, the Beneficent, the Merciful.
1.2All praise is due to Allah, the Lord of the Worlds.
1.3The Beneficent, the Merciful.
1.4Master of the Day of Judgment.
1.5Thee do we serve, and Thee do we beseech for help.
1.6Keep us on the right path.
1.7The path of those upon whom Thou hast bestowed favors. Not (the path) of those upon whom Thy wrath is brought down, nor of those who go astray.

This is as significant to the Islamic faith as the Lord's Prayer is to us. Today, take some time to pray the Prayer of Jesus, as if for the first time.

TIP

"There shall be no harm for harm, no revenge for revenge."

—The Prophet Mohammad

MONEY BACK GUARANTEE

Theme: GRACE

Order Here

When we say "unconditional," do we really mean it? If someone asks you to change who you are, recite a specific prayer, give a certain amount of money, attend a certain class for a certain number of years *before* you can receive God's unconditional love, then it's hardly unconditional is it? The flip side of grace is often harder to deal with. What would you do if you found yourself at the heavenly banquet, and according to the place cards you're sitting at the table with the girl/guy who dumped you last week? With the person who did something unspeakable to your best friend? With Osama bin Laden?

Start Thinking

Choose one.

● The instructions are on the box lid. / Hey, let's make up a new rule about hotels on Boardwalk.
● Sure, I'll go. What's in it for me? / Can we invite friends?
● Front row of the movie theater / Back row
● At the ball park, the fans and the food are the best parts. / It's all about winning.

- I want to be paid the same as everyone else. / I want to be paid more than everyone else. / I just want to be paid one dollar more than everyone else.
- I sometimes listen to the conversations of strangers around me. / That's really none of my business.

TABLE NOTES

Imagine you have to return a product you purchased at a local department store. Make a list of all the rules some stores put in place that work as "conditions" on their Unconditional Money-Back Guarantee.

SCRIPTURE MENU

Read or look up one or more of the verses, and respond to the discussion suggestions that follow.

Read 2 Corinthians 9:6–11.

Many believe that these verses refer to the "afterlife," but Jesus rarely spoke of the afterlife, though Paul did. What if this is about life on earth? How would that change things?

Do you believe in karma? Is this verse talking about a Christian version of karma?

Did you know some Christians believe that every good deed on earth is a brick for your palace in heaven? If life were about "brick earning," how would you do overall?

Have you ever given out of obligation?

Could your church survive if everyone gave out of free will? How does your church raise money?

Read Ephesians 3:8–9.

Are there any rules about Christianity that tick you off or really confuse you? Talk about them. Are these rules that you been taught or that you've understood on your own?

Have you ever been able to accept "It's just a mystery" as an answer? Would we have reached space if everyone had accepted "the mystery"? What is a great mystery that you have always wondered about?

Read Ephesians 4:1–3.

Is getting into heaven a point system? Do you think there's a trap door at the gate and certain people get dropped into hell?

Read Philippians 3:12–14.

Even Paul talked about faith as if it were an on-going process, a race without an end. Have you ever played a game just for the fun of playing?

Luke 11:9-10 (MsgB)
⁹"Here's what I'm saying:
Ask and you'll get;
Seek and you'll find;
Knock and the door will open.
¹⁰"Don't bargain with God. Be direct. Ask for what you need. This is not a cat-and-mouse, hide-and-seek game we're in.

What if "Ask, Seek, Knock" were a way of life?

Apply this to a difficult or confusing situation in your life right now. Who are you asking? What are you asking? When will you ask? What response are you hoping for?

What are you looking for (figuratively and literally)? What are you willing to give up to find it? How hard are you actually looking?

What does it take to make you knock? What other ways can you get in? What happens then?

Hebrews 11:6 (The Inclusive New Testament)
And without faith it is impossible to please God, because anyone

who comes to God must believe that God exists, rewarding those who earnestly seek the divine glory.

How is this verse an answer to the discussion questions above it?

Romans 1:19–20 (MsgB)

[19]**But the basic reality of God is plain enough. Open your eyes and there it is!** [20]**By taking a long and thoughtful look at what God has created, people have always been able to see what their eyes as such can't see: eternal power, for instance, and the mystery of his divine being. So nobody has a good excuse.**

God's answers are already there. They always have been there. What is a truth you know about God that you did not understand or could not conceive of when you were younger?

Read Matthew 20:1–16.

The last verse is a hard one for some people (the author included): "The last will be first, and the first will be last" (NIV).

Would it tick you off to see someone else get paid the same as you did when that person only did a third of the work you did? Why? If you were the one who was called at the end of the day, would you be more grateful for what you received? Why?

Is Osama bin Laden going to heaven? Is Hitler there? Would you be angry if they were? Do you think God would let you in if you were that angry and judgmental?

Before you go, read Colossians 3:12–14.

TAKE HOME BAG

Use a sheet of paper from your journal or the back of a place mat or napkin and make a coupon for Free—God's Love.

TIP

Anybody who tells you they have all the answers is either lying or selling something.

WHAT IS IT GOOD FOR?

Theme: WHY IS THERE WAR?

ORDER HERE

There is only one constant in every war ever fought: people die. Why a loving God would stand back and watch God's children annihilate each other—or even back one side over another—has been debated throughout time. What does the Bible say about war and what is the Doctrine of a Just War?

START THINKING

True or False?

- War is inevitable.
- Large bombs and larger armies are actually a deterrent to war.
- War is required to bring about change on a massive scale.
- There are no winners in war.
- If all the guns and bombs suddenly disappeared tomorrow, we'd use sticks and rocks.
- There are no atheists in foxholes.
- "It's been said that the best weapon is the one you don't have to fire. I believe that the best weapon is the one you only have to fire once."

(Tony Stark, played by Robert Downey, Jr., in the movie *Iron Man*, 2008)

TABLE NOTES

Draw a picture of a button, like on a cell phone or on a cartoon, that says "Press Here." Draw a symbol on your button that represents either death or to detonate.

Now imagine that if you pressed this button a million people might die, but we would be able to live in peace around the world for a thousand years. Could you press it?

SCRIPTURE MENU

Many scholars believe in the thirteenth century Saint Thomas Aquinas laid the groundwork for what would become the doctrine of a "just war"—conditions that make it acceptable in the eyes of God to fight a war. To be considered "just," a war had to:

1. Be the last resort
2. Have a just cause
3. Have legitimate authority
4. Have a right purpose

Thomas Aquinas said that war was justified only if it contributed to the common good. Do you think the "common good" can be confined to any one nation or people? Explain.

Martin Luther and Saint Augustine both felt that violence for self-defense wasn't acceptable but violence for defending others was. Do you agree?

To what standard do we hold ourselves for violence to be acceptable?

Exodus 20:13 (KJV)
Thou shalt not kill.

"Not kill" in this verse comes from the Hebrew word *ratsach*, (raw-tskah') which means "dash to pieces," as in murder. Do you think God differentiates between "kill" and "murder"? Does our culture?

Have you ever found yourself on the opposite side of popular opinion? How did that feel?

Ecclesiastes 3:8 (NIV)
"a time to love and a time to hate,
a time for war and a time for peace."

As of this book's publication in 2008, the United States is still at war in Iraq. What is the status of that war as you read this? When the war began, the majority of Americans were in favor of going to war. Feelings about the war changed over the years the war continued. When did the change occur? If this book is being used years from now, what has hindsight brought that we didn't know when this book was published?

Does God cause war? Read these passages:

Exodus 17:16
Numbers 21:3, 31:1-2
Deuteronomy 2:33, 3:3, 7:1-2
1 Samuel 15:1-3
2 Samuel 23:10

It seems that God was actively involved in the battles from the Old Testament. Do you think God chose sides or that the stories were written by the winners? Explain.

How do we say "God is on our side" today?

Psalm 46:9 (TNCH)

God makes wars cease to the end of the earth;
God breaks the bow and shatters the spear;
God burns the shields with fire.

Why do you think that God does not stop wars? Why doesn't God just shoot beams out of his eyes and melt all the weapons at once?

Matthew 5:39 (NRSV)
"But I say to you, Do not resist an evildoer. But if anyone strikes you on the right cheek, turn the other also...."

What would Jesus do? Answer it as best you can.

Read Ecclesiastes 9:14–17.
Rewrite verse 17 as if it were going to be a bumper sticker on your car.

Isaiah 2:4 (NIV)
He will judge between the nations
and will settle disputes for many peoples.
They will beat their swords into plowshares
and their spears into pruning hooks.
Nation will not take up sword against nation,
nor will they train for war anymore.

Do "guns for shoes" programs work? (Substitute for "shoes" according to any program you've heard of.) Would "swords for shovels" work?

TAKE HOME BAG

Can you think of reasons or a doctrine for a "just peace"? Write them down here. Try sending them to your congressional representative and see what response you get.

TIP

"Technology will save us...if it doesn't wipe us out first."

—Pete Seeger

FALLING DOWN

THEME: TRAGEDY

ORDER HERE

On September 11, 2001, madmen flew planes into the towers of the World Trade Center in New York and into the Pentagon in Washington, D.C. Somewhere else in the world, a mother held the hand of her child who slowly succumbed to the AIDS virus. Children starve to death. People disappear between the door of their building and the car. (Sometimes the bodies are found, sometimes they are not.) In a world like this, how do we keep on believing?

START THINKING

Choose one.

- The hurricane happened because God was angry. / The weather conditions were favorable for hurricane activity.
- If I had know X was going to happen I would have been able to avoid it. / X would have happened no matter what.
- Adam Sandler comedy / Shakespearean tragedy

- "Sad is like happy for deep people" (Stephen Moffat). / Let a smile be your umbrella.
- I want answers and I want them now. / It's something I just don't get to know.

TABLE NOTES

On a piece of paper or the back of a place mat...

- Mark a period.
- Make a short list of things in your life that have ended recently.
- Make an exclamation point.
- Then make another list of things that have ended very suddenly and very badly.

SCRIPTURE MENU

Read or look up one or more of the verses, and respond to the discussion suggestions that follow.

Read Psalm 22:1–5.

This was the Psalm Jesus quoted from the cross. When was a time in your life where you felt completely and totally abandoned by God?

Romans 5:3–5 (NIV)

³Not only so, but we also rejoice in our sufferings, because we know that suffering produces perseverance; ⁴perseverance, character; and character, hope. ⁵And hope does not disappoint us, because God has poured out his love into our hearts by the Holy Spirit, whom he has given us.

Have you ever had someone tell you to "look on the bright side"? How did you (want to) respond? What can we often tell about a bad time in our lives down the road that we can't tell while we are in it? What keeps us from seeing the bigger picture?

That being said, is the passage from Romans 5 true?

Has someone ever asked you, "Why did God allows this to happen?" What did you say? Pretend it has happened right now, what would you tell someone?

In the Bible a man named Job loses absolutely everything. Job weeps and praises God. Could you do that?

What's the worst that could happen? Seriously, think about your life. In terms of your life individually or we as a country or we as a planet...what's the worst thing that could happen?

Romans 8:27–29 (NIV)

²⁷And he who searches our hearts knows the mind of the Spirit, because the Spirit intercedes for the saints in accordance with God's will.
²⁸And we know that in all things God works for the good of those who love him, who have been called according to his purpose. ²⁹For those God foreknew he also predestined to be conformed to the likeness of his Son, that he might be the firstborn among many brothers.

The Bible says "all things", not "some things" or "the things that are in America's best interest." The Bible says ALL things, good and bad. All things happen so that we can be closer to God.

Read 2 Corinthians 1:3–7.

When you are hurting, do you like to be alone or have people around you?

September 11th united this nation as it hadn't been united in years. Is it important for our souls (individually and collectively) to suffer collectively? Why or why not?

Mel Brooks said, "Tragedy is when I cut my finger. Comedy is when you walk into an open sewer and die." Is it true that tragedy is only a tragedy when it happens to us?

In times of tragedy many Christians turn to the Psalm 23. Do you think this is out of tradition or something more spiritual? Why?

TAKE HOME BAG

Read Job 38: 4–18.

This is a long rant from God in answer to Job's "Why God why?" prayer. Think about something that's going on in your life or something that has been on your soul for awhile. Then read these verses again.

Two Rules to remember:

1. God is God.
2. You are not God.

RIGHT TURN ONLY

THEME: THE ONLY WAY

ORDER HERE

When we total it up, the majority of the world is not Christian. (Forget about the way Christians divide themselves.) Do we really think that when Jesus said "only through me" he meant that only a relatively small portion of the population was "getting in"? How do we reconcile a God of unconditional love with a "turn or burn" theology?

START THINKING

Choose one.

- "Road Closed" simply means go around the sign. / Take the detour and avoid car damage.
- There are guarantees in life. / Everything happens by chance.
- I'd rather be the pie / the pie pan / the ingredients.
- I'd rather sit in church next to my parents / next to a drag queen.

- I'd rather play euchre / Shoots and Ladders.™
- The book of Leviticus / the Ten Commandments / Love God. Love each other.
- Watch a building go up / Watch a building come down
- Watch *The Ten Commandments* / Watch *Dogma* / Watch *The Passion of the Christ*.
- Read the menu / Look at what others around me are eating

TABLE NOTES

Draw a dot in the middle of a blank piece of paper or on the back of a place mat. Now close your eyes and try to drop your pencil point on the exact same dot. Try several times. Try it once while keeping your eyes closed and moving the paper back and forth. Open your eyes and see how close you came.

How is this activity like the way some people view their chances of getting into heaven?

SCRIPTURE MENU

Read aloud or look up one or more of the verses, and respond to the discussion suggestions that follow.

John 14:6 (NRSV)

Jesus said to him, "I am the way, and the truth, and the life. No one comes to the Father except through me."

Break this verse into its three parts:

the way
the truth
the life

Jesus spoke in symbolism all the time. If we are on a spiritual journey, how do these words apply?

Read John 1:1–5.

God is. God was. God always will be. Everything is part of God. How are these words of comfort for those who believe they will never "get in"?

Read Deuteronomy 29:29.

We don't know everything. Can we ask what are the things we don't know? Not really, because then we would know them. Have you ever had to deal with someone who claims to know everything about a subject? What do such people have in common with one another? What is the best way to get along with these people?

Have you ever been working on a paper or art project and have someone tell you that you are doing it wrong? Can creativity ever be wrong?

Read Romans 2:12–16.

If we believe in the grace of God—that is, that God loves us and welcomes us no matter what—is that a permission slip to live however we want to? Explain.

Romans 1:19-20 (MsgB)
But the basic reality of God is plain enough. Open your eyes and there it is!

If this is the basic reality of God, how can some people not see it? Why do others want it to be complicated?

Hebrews 11:6 (MsgB)
It's impossible to please God apart from faith. And why? Because anyone who wants to approach God must believe both that he exists and that he cares enough to respond to those who seek him.

Just because God is angry, does that mean you don't "get in"? Have you ever acted like your parents don't exist? Did they still love you?

Psalm 105:43 (TNCH)
So God brought god's people out with joy
**   God's chosen ones with singing.**

The Bible refers to the Jewish people as God's "chosen" people over and over again. If the Jews are already "chosen," why would God need to send Jesus?

Jesus talks about "the kingdom" as satisfaction. Jesus uses water as an analogy many times, such as here: "You're hot and sweaty. I'm water." There's no coercion involved. Have you ever hung out with someone who treated his or her belief as if it were a license to straighten other people out?

Romans 11:6 (NIV)
And if by grace, then it is no longer by works; if it were, grace would no longer be grace.

You can't put conditions on what's unconditional. Talk about a time when someone tried to put a "however," an "as long as," or an "except" on you or someone you knew.

1 John 3:9 (MsgB)
People conceived and brought into life by God don't make a practice of sin. How could they? God's seed is deep within them, making them who they are. It's not in the nature of the God-begotten to practice and parade sin.

Read John 3:1–8.

Have you ever noticed that the people who have the most problem understanding Jesus' message are the ones who try to take it literally?

Notice that Jesus talks about "the wind" in verse 8. The Holy Spirit is "the wind." It's the Holy Spirit that seems to do the choosing. We humans can't choose to be born anew; that's the Spirit's job.

Matthew's Gospel uses the term "regeneration," which literally means "new birth." This word is used in Titus 3:5 to mean a change of heart. What does it mean in 1 John 3:14, 2 Corinthians 5:17 (take note "Dr. Who" fans), and

Romans 2:12?

When you think of a "born again Christian," what usually comes to mind? What if we were to look at being "born again" like one of the above passages?

TAKE HOME BAG

Go back to your piece of paper you made a dot on. Draw a large circle the whole way around the piece of paper, and see if you can drop the pencil point within the circle. This is grace.

TIP

Ask. Seek. Knock. It's what being a Christian is about.

DECISIONS, DECISIONS

THEME: FREE WILL

ORDER HERE

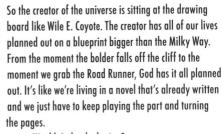

So the creator of the universe is sitting at the drawing board like Wile E. Coyote. The creator has all of our lives planned out on a blueprint bigger than the Milky Way. From the moment the bolder falls off the cliff to the moment we grab the Road Runner, God has it all planned out. It's like we're living in a novel that's already written and we just have to keep playing the part and turning the pages.

Wouldn't that be boring?

God gave us Free Will. We get to choose. Left or Right. Paper or Plastic. Regular or Decaf. Yet at the same time God calls us, guides us, makes us co-creators in God's creation, the creation of an ever expanding universe and the creation of ourselves.

START THINKING

True or False?

- I have at least one movie memorized from beginning to end.
- To me, a vacation does not require a map, a timetable, or an agenda.
- I once read the last chapter or page of a book just because I wanted to know how it ended.
- I will hunt for my gifts before Christmas.
- The person I will marry has been pre-determined. I just have to find him/her.

- I'd rather shop on eBay than at the mall.
- I could leave a lottery scratch-off ticket as a tip for a waiter/waitress.

Finish the thought.

- If I could live inside any TV show, it would be...

TABLE NOTES

Draw a circle, square, or triangle in the space below.

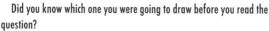

Did you know which one you were going to draw before you read the question?

Did God know which one you were going to draw before you read the question?

SCRIPTURE MENU

Read or look up one or more of the verses, and respond to the discussion suggestions that follow.

Genesis 1:27 (NRSV)

So God created humankind in his image, in the image of God he created them; male and female he created them.

If we are created in the image of God, what does that say about God? Are we creative? Occasionally unsure? Unaware of our destiny?

We as a species are constantly evolving and changing. What if the same is true of God? Is it scary to think of God constantly evolving and changing?

Isaiah 43:1–2 (NRSV)

¹But now thus says the Lord, he who created you, O Jacob, he who formed you, O Israel: Do not fear, for I have redeemed you; I have

called you by name, you are mine. ²When you pass through the waters, I will be with you; and through the rivers, they shall not overwhelm you; when you walk through fire you shall not be burned, and the flame shall not consume you.

If we belong to God from the beginning, will our bad choices ever keep us from God?

Read John 17:22–23.

God is one with the universe. God and Jesus are one. Jesus wants us to be one with him, as he is one with God. Are we connected to the universe in all time in all things? Are we part of the past present and future?

Do you believe that God knows what your great-grandchild will name her cat?

Romans 5:20–6:2 (NIV)

²⁰The law was added so that the trespass might increase. But where sin increased, grace increased all the more, ²¹so that, just as sin reigned in death, so also grace might reign through righteousness to bring eternal life through Jesus Christ our Lord.

⁶:¹What shall we say, then? Shall we go on sinning so that grace may increase? ²By no means! We died to sin; how can we live in it any longer?

1 Corinthians 13:11 (NRSV)

When I was a child, I spoke like a child, I thought like a child, I reasoned like a child; when I became an adult, I put an end to childish ways.

When you were a child, who was in charge of you? Who planned your sleep, your meals, your sleeping, your rising? At what point did you start getting yourself out of bed and picking out your own clothes? At what point does "grown-up" begin?

Looking at humankind as an "adult," at what point do we get to make our own choices?

How good are you at making decisions? Has there ever been a point where you wished a decision wasn't entirely yours? Talk about that.

Galatians 5:13 (NRSV)

For you were called to freedom, brothers and sisters; only do not use your freedom as an opportunity for self-indulgence, but through love become slaves to one another.

We have choices. We can cherish one another or we can kill one another.

You can make the conscious choice not to do your homework. Then what happens?

1 Peter 2:9 (The Inclusive New Testament)
You, however, are a chosen people, a royal priesthood, a conse-crated nation, a people set apart to sing the praises of the One who called you out of the darkness into the wonderful, divine light.

What if we choose to live our lives the way God wants us to live our lives as a way of saying "thank you" for our lives?

If a waiter or waitress goes out of the way to give you great service, don't we pay that service back with a better tip and maybe a return to the restaurant? How many people do you know who would get amazing service and great food and then stiff the server?

Who is the server in this analogy, us or God?

Read 1 John 3:2.

TAKE HOME BAG

Draw a puzzle piece on a blank piece of paper or on the back of a place mat.

Part of the discussion of having Free Will has to be the idea that for all our intelligence and faith, we are still only seeing one little piece of a massive puzzle.

God is seeing the big picture. When was the last time you put together a puzzle? How is that like life?

God knew you were going to read this. Good choice.

WANT TO HEAR A FUNNY YOKE?

Theme: RULES

Order Here

Have you ever played with Silly Putty,™ that small bit of goo that comes in a plastic egg? You can stretch it and break it. You can mold it into a dog or a bouncy ball. You can use it to pick up pictures off the newspaper. If you leave it alone and don't play with it or forget to put it away, it's pretty much worthless as a toy. It's meant to keep being changed into something new. What if this is how our relationship with God works? What if the debate about what is good and what is not good is built into the process?

Start Thinking

Always, sometimes, or never?

- I leave generous tips at coffee shops.
- I will choose a cereal or a Happy Meal™ if the prize is cool.
- I can a laugh at my mistakes.
- I say "thank you."
- I belch in front of my grandmother.
- I treat my parents like they love me.
- I put my change in the charity box.
- I roll my windows down when my favorite song is playing.
- I close the cereal bag in the box.
- I remember my friends' birthdays.
- I study for finals.

TABLE NOTES

On a piece of paper or the back of a place mat...

- Draw a simple seesaw. Off to the side make a column of the Ten Commandments (Exodus 20).
- Label one side of the seesaw "Oh my gosh yes!" Label the other side "Ehh...not so much."
- "Stack" the commandments on the seesaw any way you want. You can adjust the "weight" of the commandments. See if you can come up with a balance.

SCRIPTURE MENU

Let's imagine that your denomination teaches that you must be in church every single Sunday. If you miss a Sunday service, God will be very mad. Now let's imagine that it's Sunday morning and your mother calls you on the phone and says, "The car broke down, I'm stuck in a parking lot, you have to come get me." The Bible says you must honor your parents, but it also says keep the Sabbath holy. Which do you do, rescue your mom or go to church?

Read Mark 3:1–6.

There are 613 commandments in the book of Leviticus. The big ten are not the only ones that people were expected to follow. The commandments often contradict each other. Rabbis at the time would choose which ones were "heavier" and which ones were "lighter." People would choose a rabbi to follow based on that rabbi's list.

Romans 7:6 (MsgB)
But now that we're no longer shackled to that domineering mate of sin, and out from under all those oppressive regulations and fine print, we're free to live a new life in the freedom of God.

What are the most "sacred" rules in your church that have nothing to do with Jesus or the Bible?

This verse from Romans seems to be saying that following Jesus is to get out from under the strain of all the rules. Do you have a list of rules posted anywhere in your church?

Read John 3:8.

According to Jesus, the Holy Spirit moves like the wind. (How many different analogies can you make out of that one?) Do we cause the presence of the Holy Spirit? Can we make it do what we want?

Is the presence of God affected by our following the rules at all? What are they there for?

Matthew 6:33 (The Inclusive New Testament)
Seek first God's reign, and God's justice, and all these things will be given to you besides.

If we were to "seek first" what God wanted of us and *then* went and did what we thought was right, would we still get in trouble? With whom?

Does WWJD work?

Does WWJD hurt?

Read 2 Corinthians 6:4–5.

Ephesians 4:1–3 (NIV)
[1]As a prisoner for the Lord, then, I urge you to live a life worthy of the calling you have received. [2]Be completely humble and gentle; be patient, bearing with one another in love. [3]Make every effort to keep the unity of the Spirit through the bond of peace.

Have you ever worshipped in a church outside of your denomination? Have you ever worshipped in a place of worship outside of your religion? Was it more fascinating or uncomfortable? Why?

Churches have split over issues as simple as using wine or grape juice in communion. What is the biggest (heaviest) thing your church has had to deal with? How did it survive?

When rabbis chose which commandments were heavier and which were lighter, they would take these commandments on and refer to them as a yoke.

Matthew 11:28-30 (NRSV)

28"Come to me, all you that are weary and are carrying heavy burdens, and I will give you rest. 29Take my yoke upon you, and learn from me; for I am gentle and humble in heart, and you will find rest for your souls. 30For my yoke is easy, and my burden is light."

To whom is Jesus offering the "yoke"? (Okay, you can re-read the verse, but that's not the answer.) To whom does Jesus offer the yoke?

Is Jesus' yoke easy? Explain.

Jesus is giving the disciples the "keys" (the permission, the power) to interpret the scripture as to which is heavier and which is lighter. If we see the Bible as a history or a textbook, it will be hard to see it any other way. If we see the Bible as a living and breathing presence in our lives, it will continue to loosen and bind and speak to all of us.

If the Bible can be loosened and bound, that allows God to speak to us through those words this day, right here, right now. What is God saying? How are we reacting?

Take Home Bag

How heavy is your yoke? What heavy rules do you carry around that you just can't get out from under? This week pray to God and be willing to give them up and carry what God hands you.

Tip

Jesus summed up all 613 commandments in just two.
Love God.
Love each other.
Are those the heaviest or lightest of all?

A MIGHTY WIND

14 THEME: HOLY SPIRIT

ORDER HERE

One third of the Trinity, the Holy Spirit, is God's continued presence on earth. First there was God, then God became flesh and blood (that's Jesus), and then Jesus said, "I'm outta here, but I'm going to leave you a guide." The Holy Spirit is that guide. It is the source of inspiration and comfort. It is the movement of God over the water. It is a source and a presence and reminder.

START THINKING

Choose one.

- Read a map / Ask Someone for directions
- Follow the recipe / Cook with someone who knows the recipe
- Add the numbers in my head / Use a calculator
- Learn by watching / Learn by doing
- Touch it to see if it's hot / If it looks hot and smells hot, that's good enough for me.

Table Notes

Visual images of the Holy Spirit include a mighty wind, a soft breeze, a gentle voice, a dove, and a tongue of fire. All of these are to signify the presence of God. Use this space to draw a picture of the Holy Spirit. You can use one of the traditional images or create your own to symbolize how the presence was present in your life.

Scripture Menu

Read or look up one or more of the verses, and respond to the discussion suggestions that follow.

2 Timothy 1:14 (NIV)
Guard the good deposit that was entrusted to you—guard it with the help of the Holy Spirit who lives in us.

Read Jeremiah 31:31–34.

Through the Spirit, God is present at all times and in all places. If God is here all the time, how do we connect to the Spirit? Have you ever "invited" the connection?

Have you ever had one of those perfect moments late at night on a mission trip or driving with your window down and a favorite song on the radio?

Talk about a time that you felt "connected."

Read John 16:1–7.

What does Jesus tell the disciples about the Holy Spirit? Are these conditions?

John 20:19-23 (NRSV)

[19]When it was evening on that day, the first day of the week, and the doors of the house where the disciples had met were locked for fear of the Jews, Jesus came and stood among them and said, "Peace be with you." [20]After he said this, he showed them his hands and his side. Then the disciples rejoiced when they saw the Lord. [21]Jesus said to them again, "Peace be with you. As the Father has sent me, so I send you." [22]When he had said this, he breathed on them and said to them, "Receive the Holy Spirit. [23]If you forgive the sins of any, they are forgiven them; if you retain the sins of any, they are retained."

What do you think the Holy Spirit sounds like? Smells like?

Acts 2:37-47 (NRSV)

[37]Now when they heard this, they were cut to the heart and said to Peter and to the other apostles, "Brothers, what should we do?" [38]Peter said to them, "Repent, and be baptized every one of you in the name of Jesus Christ so that your sins may be forgiven; and you will receive the gift of the Holy Spirit. [39]For the promise is for you, for your children, and for all who are far away, everyone whom the Lord our God calls to him." [40]And he testified with many other arguments and exhorted them, saying, "Save yourselves from this corrupt generation." [41]So those who welcomed his message were baptized, and that day about three thousand persons were added. [42]They devoted themselves to the apostles' teaching and fellowship, to the breaking of bread and the prayers.

[43]Awe came upon everyone, because many wonders and signs were being done by the apostles. [44]All who believed were together and had all things in common; [45]they would sell their possessions and goods and distribute the proceeds to all, as any had need. [46]Day by day, as they spent much time together in the temple, they broke bread at home and ate their food with glad and generous hearts, [47]praising God and having the goodwill of all the people. And day by day the Lord added to their number those who were being saved.

This passage is commonly known as the "birth of the church." The Holy Spirit was present then and is present right now. The same spirit that passed through the disciples is in this place. How does that make you feel?

When the Holy Spirit looks at what the church as become since its creation, do you think the Spirit is dancing or crying or something else?

Read 1 Corinthians 12:4–11.

The word "spirit" comes from the same place we get the word "inspiration." Inspiration is from God through the Holy Spirit. Can we say that the same Spirit that inspired Handel to write the *Messiah*, that inspired Beethoven to write his symphonies, also inspired Billy Joe Armstrong to write *American Idiot*? Why or why not?

TAKE HOME BAG

Each of the words below is taken from the Bible in reference to what the Holy Spirit does for us. Circle three of the words that describe how the Holy Spirit has acted for you. Write a sentence of two about that moment.

Seals	Fills
Recognizes	Authorizes
Intercedes	Renews
Inspires	Reveals
Teaches	Directs
Enables	Reminds
Promises	Binds

"Water is an individual, an animal, and is alive; remove the hydrogen and *it* is an animal and is alive; the remaining oxygen is also an individual, an animal, and is alive. Recapitulation: the two individuals combined, constitute a third individual—and yet each *continues* to be an individual... Here was mute Nature explaining the sublime mystery of the Trinity so luminously that even the commonest understanding could comprehend it, whereas many a trained master of words had labored to do it with speech and failed."

—Mark Twain, in "Three Thousand Years Among the Microbes"

ENGRAVED INVITATION

Theme: THE PRODIGAL SON

Order Here

Each and every one of us is capable of doing and accomplishing wonderful things. Each and every one of us is also capable of doing incredibly nasty things to one another. The parable of the Prodigal Son is not so much a story about sibling rivalry as it about coming to grips with who we are and what we are capable of.

Start Thinking

Choose one. I prefer...

- To throw plates / spin plates
- Dribble a basketball / Spin a basketball on my finger
- Swings / Seesaw
- The first 20 minutes of *The Wizard of Oz* / The last 2 hours of *Oz*
- Black and white / Twenty different shades of blue
- Swimming / Surfing / Diving

TABLE NOTES

Draw the side view of a large pig. Use dotted lines to divide the pig into sections, as on a butcher shop's poster. Now label each of those sections with some of the large and small mistakes you've made recently.

SCRIPTURE MENU

Read or look up one or more of the verses, and respond to the discussion suggestions that follow.

Read Luke 5: 11–32.

Look again at verses 17–19. Have you ever practiced what you were going to say to your parents when you KNEW you were in deep, deep trouble? Talk about that.

Notice in verse 21 that the young son leaves out the part about "make me one of your hired hands." Would you stop confessing if you knew forgiveness was already given?

Many times when this story is read or appears in Sunday school books for younger children, verses 28–32 are left out. Yet these verses are important, too. Do you think the older son went into the party at the end of the story?

Why do you suppose Jesus didn't "finish" the story?

If we end the story at verse 27, we have a nice little package. Why do you think so many Christians want to have Jesus nicely packaged?

Usually the big idea we take away is to be the good son and not the bad son. What if we are both? What if the father in the story is God calling us (both our good and bad sides) to the same party? How does that change the story?

Remember the images (usually in cartoons) of a person with the angel on one shoulder and a devil on the other? Who is in the middle? We have these struggles all the time, but we must accept that both are a part of us.

What if the father is God who is asking us not to be good, but to be whole?

TAKE HOME BAG

Use a piece of paper or part of the place mat to make a party invitation. Decorate it, fold it—whatever you wish. Put your name on the outside and the letters RSVP on the inside. Keep this with you this week, and think about what it means to accept the invitation.

TIP

"I'd rather be whole than good."

—Karl Jung

TALENT SHOW

THEME: THE KING + THE TALENTS

ORDER HERE

Imagine chocolate. Sweet chocolate. The best kind in the world. Better than that, imagine chocolate from heaven. Chocolate made by angels. All of it in one big box. You don't have to poke any of them, because they are all going to be wonderful. God hands you this box. Are you going to hog it all or are you going to share? *Hint:* Choose sharing.

As soon as you begin sharing, you notice that the box does not get empty. You can throw fistfuls of it out to a crowd, and the box will still be full. If you horde it, shove it in a drawer, or hide it under your bed, you will start to notice a certain bitterness and the names of the candies will change from Chocolate-Peanut-Butter-Whoopie to things like Crunchy Frog.

START THINKING

Choose one.

● Which one gets better as time goes by?

Wine / Cheese / Wisdom / Sex / Creative ability / All of the above.

● I'll play my music for my family / myself / my school / on live television.

- When the column of numbers adds up the way they should, that's pure luck / a symphony.
- My dreams are realistic / colorful / explosive / corrosive.

Fill in the blank:
- When I was a little kid, I wanted to be a(n) _____
  _____ when I grew up.

TABLE NOTES

In the space below or on the back of a place mat, draw a picture of a coin. If your "talents" were coins what would they look like? You can draw more than one coin if you wish.

SCRIPTURE MENU

Read or look up one or more of the verses, and respond to the discussion suggestions that follow.

*Read the parable of the talents, Matthew 25:14–30.
Then read 1 Corinthians 12:4–11.*

What do you notice about these two passages?

Look closely at verse 28 of the Matthew passage. What is this man's view of the king? If, in this parable, the king is God...then what is the modern-day equivalent of verse 28?

We have all been given gifts. Something divine, something "of God" has been put into each of us. Why is this hard to believe for some people?

We have a divine responsibility to use the gift for the common good. We have a divine responsibility to share the chocolate.

Ecclesiastes 10:10 (NIV)
If the ax is dull
   and its edge unsharpened,
more strength is needed
   but skill will bring success.

How does this verse apply to the talents that God has given us?

Do you know someone who has buried her or his gifts in the dirt?

Romans 5:1–5 (NRSV)
¹Therefore, since we are justified by faith, we have peace with God through our Lord Jesus Christ, ²through whom we have obtained access to this grace in which we stand; and we boast in our hope of sharing the glory of God. ³And not only that, but we also boast in our sufferings, knowing that suffering produces endurance, ⁴and endurance produces character, and character produces hope, ⁵and hope does not disappoint us, because God's love has been poured into our hearts through the Holy Spirit that has been given to us.

How can suffering be a gift?

2 Corinthians 6:4–5 (NRSV)
⁴But as servants of God we have commended ourselves in every way: through great endurance, in afflictions, hardships, calamities, ⁵beatings, imprisonments, riots, labors, sleepless nights, hunger....

The word "commend" in this passage is translated from the Greek word *sunistao* (soon-is-tah-oh), which means to strengthen. We "strengthen" one another in our troubles and hardships and at all our bad times. How do we do this?

If we all have a divine gift from God and we choose to bury it in the dirt, what happens to those around us?

God made you completely and totally unique. Look around: is there anyone else in the room who is just like you? Now think about this: What if *you* are the gift. Not as in, "Jenny can sing, she must have a gift." What if Jenny *is* the gift? What if *you* are the gift, the talent, that God has given? As a group, what do we do with you?

Colossians 3:23 (NRSV)
Whatever your task, put yourselves into it, as done for the Lord and not for your masters....

Read 1 Corinthians 3:10–17.

Fire in the scripture is not about destruction—it's about refinement. If we are building the church (not the physical building but *the* church, as in the body of Christ), what are we building with?

Take Home Bag

Write a note on a piece of paper or on the back of a place mat. Draw a heart. It's a "gift card" to go on your box of chocolates. Write a note from God to the world about you.

You are a unique and individual and totally relevant creation of a creator and creating God. And God has made you a partner in the creative process that is you.

   Got that? Read it again.

BALLPARK MUSTARD

THEME: FAITH THE SIZE OF A MUSTARD SEED

ORDER HERE

The disciples constantly ask Jesus about faith for all the wrong reasons. They argue over who is the greatest among them. James and John's mother actually comes to a meeting and tries to guilt Jesus into setting a special place at the table for her boys. Jesus understood that the disciples didn't have clue about what they were asking. He understood that their faith had to grow. He knew some of them wouldn't fully believe until he came back from the dead (and some of them not even then.) Jesus knows that faith is a process. It happens as we grow and mature.

START THINKING

Fill in the blank.

● The age at which I stopped believing in the Easter Bunny:

● The age at which I learned to read:

- The age at which I was fully potty trained:

- The age at which I first drove a car:

- The age at which I stopped getting the Happy Meal™:

- The age at which I knew God was more than the white guy with the beard I saw in the Sunday school books:

Table Notes

On a blank piece of paper, draw a dot. If you are at a coffee shop, shake just a little bit of pepper out of the shaker. See if you can separate it so you have just one grain of pepper. Draw a circle around it so you can now see where it is.

This is the size of a mustard seed. Yet it eventually becomes the most popular of all spices in ballparks around the country.

Scripture Menu

We'll start with Luke, and then we'll work backward and forward from this passage.

Luke 17:5–6 (NIV)
⁵The apostles said to the Lord, "Increase our faith!"

⁶He replied, "If you have faith as small as a mustard seed, you can say to this mulberry tree, 'Be uprooted and planted in the sea,' and it will obey you."

First, get that amazing image in your head. Is it like a cartoon in which the branches of the tree reach out and pull up its own roots and then the tree does a cannonball dive into the seat—"Whoopeeee." Or it's like one of those "Special FX" shots, in which Jesus aims his palms at the tree and the disciples feel the ground shake and, suddenly, with just a motion of telekinesis, Jesus hurls the tree into the ocean, like he's on "Heroes."

Which image suits you? Jesus tells the disciples they already have the power to do this.

Jesus' line about moving the tree is in response to the disciples asking for more faith. Whatever faith they have, they want more. Jesus tells them that it's not about how much faith they have but about its sincerity.

If you could look closely at the original Greek, you would find that the disciples are not necessarily asking for faith. They are asking for power. They want to do the "water into wine" trick. They want to heal others. They want to walk on water. They want what Jesus has.

Notice also that the disciples think they already have faith and just want Jesus to increase it. So Jesus tells them a story about a servant and a master.

Read Luke 17:7–10.

The disciples want to be like Jesus, and Jesus says that being a servant is its own reward. You don't go work at a homeless shelter on a Saturday and then spend Monday telling everyone at school what you did. You did your job. You did your bit. That's enough.

Is it hard not to take credit even when credit is due? Is there anything wrong with wanting a pat on the back once in awhile?

For Jesus, being a servant is a way of life. Jesus' last act with the disciples is to wash the muck from between their toes while knowing full well that he's going to be killed tomorrow.

What is genuine faith?

Is it hard to accept things on faith? Why do you suppose that we are a culture that must see it, hear it, taste it, and smell it before we believe?

It seems like every year about Easter time someone comes out with a new documentary on Jesus' bones or a new "lost" Gospel. Some Christians immediately discount the discovery, while others embrace it as a chance to say, "See? Here's your proof." Have you ever wanted proof of God? Have you ever said something like, "Okay God, if you are really, really there then you will..."

Hebrews 11:1 (NIV)
Now faith is being sure of what we hope for and certain of what we do not see.

The verse from Hebrews says that's exactly what faith is—belief without proof. How do you show your faith?

Did you have a "lights and fog" type experience, or was your belief a slow process?

How as your faith grown in the past few years? What were some of the triggers?

How big is a mustard seed?

Have you ever had mustard at the ballpark? Is it better than the stuff you buy in the store? There are people who don't eat mustard outside of a stadium, but once they get inside they put in on their dog with a paint roller. How is this like your faith life?

What is the "ballpark" in your life? Where are you and what are you doing when your faith is the strongest?

TAKE HOME BAG

Look at a menu, or look in your refrigerator at home. Choose another food item and create your own faith analogy. Write it down and bring it to the next session.

_____

You can move mountains. It might be one stone at a time, but all it takes is a little faith (and a lot of patience.)

THE BODY + THE BLOOD

Theme: COMMUNION

ORDER HERE

Communion is a ritual. Yet it is more than a ritual. For some, it is a sacred practice taught to them by people who had it taught to them by people who had it taught to them by Jesus Christ. The ritual of communion began with Jesus and friends after the Passover celebration. It is a ritual that has changed since then. When we "take" the bread and the wine, we are performing the action almost the same way as Jesus did on the night he was arrested.

START THINKING

True or False?

- I believe in angels.
- I believe in luck.
- I can enjoy a magic show without trying to figure out how it's done.
- I can color without lines on my paper.
- If the sign says "Wet Paint," I'm the kind of person who will touch it to be sure.

- If scientists tell me that the light I see in the stars actually started out billions of years ago, I will believe them.
- I believe men walked on the moon.
- A white coat and a clipboard adds a lot to a person's authority.
- A white collar or a long robe adds a lot to a person's authority.

Question: If the label on the outside of the peanut butter jar says "Crunchy," what makes your believe that the peanut butter on the inside is crunchy?

Table Notes

Everything about the communion meal has meaning. The bread is broken, held, shared, and eaten. The wine is poured, held up, shared, and drunk. Draw a simple place setting. Think of a bigger meaning for each of the items on the place mat.

SCRIPTURE MENU

Here's the longest word in the whole book, ready? Transubstantiation. This word means a change in the reality of a substance. Look at your shoe. Your shoe has a shape, but the shape is not the shoe. Your shoe has a color, but the color is not the shoe.

Some churches believe that during the act of communion the "substance" of the bread and the wine "transfigures" into the actual blood and body of Jesus Christ. Other churches believe that the act of taking the bread and the wine is a sacred ritual in which the items are symbols of the body and the blood. Some churches only allow ordained clergy to lead communion, while others allow anyone to lead the ritual.

For too many churches, the ritual has become an oft-repeated ceremony of Wonder Bread™ and Welch's™ and has little meaning

Read Exodus 12:21–32.

The story of Passover is from the book of Exodus. The Israelites were still slaves when the "Passover" occurred, but they were preparing to be freed. When the Passover meal is celebrated, it is done with shoes on and bread baked quickly as recognition of the idea that the Jews were about to leave. This is the meal that Jesus and the disciples were celebrating just before what we've come to know as the Last Supper.

What is the biggest "ritual" meal in your family? When is it? Are there special foods or prayers? Is there a ritual in your family that has been repeated since before your parents were born and will undoubtedly be practiced when your great-grandchildren are old?

Another word for communion in some denominations is Eucharist, which means "thanksgiving." How is communion like what we know as Thanksgiving? (*Hint: What did Jesus do when he picked up the bread?*)

What does it take to make something sacred?

Are there rules about communion in your church?

Have you ever made your own Christmas gifts for family or friends? What if you wanted to give someone a gift and you didn't even have any stuff to make something with? What would you give?

Jesus did not specifically choose the bread and the wine. Jesus used what was on hand after the Passover meal. Do you think communion could be celebrated with Oreos™ and milk?

When Jesus said "body and blood," he would have used these two words together. In Aramaic, Jesus said *bisra udema*. Both are words used in sacrificial ceremonies, and both refer to a death that is violent and bloody.

1 Corinthians 5:7-8 (MsgB)
So get rid of this "yeast." Our true identity is flat and plain, not puffed up with the wrong kind of ingredient. The Messiah, our Passover Lamb, has already been sacrificed for the Passover meal, and we are the Unraised Bread part of the Feast. ⁸So let's live out our part in the Feast, not as raised bread swollen with the yeast of evil, but as flat bread—simple, genuine, unpretentious.

Have you ever heard Jesus referred to as "the Passover Lamb"? Early Christians made the association of Jesus' Last Supper to the Passover meal. Jesus is the sacrificed lamb. We are the bread made without yeast. Yeast in this verse is seen as a bad thing. What are some of the "yeasts" in our lives that make us full of ourselves?

John 17:21 (MsgB)
**The goal is for all of them to become one heart and mind—
Just as you, Father, are in me and I in you,
So they might be one heart and mind with us.
Then the world might believe that you, in fact,
    sent me.**

Jesus prayed this prayer just after the last supper. Jesus was letting the disciples know that by "taking him in" they were in fact "one with him" and one with God.

When have you felt like you were "one with God"? When was the last time you had a "perfect moment"?

What do you do that while you are doing it you think, "I could do this forever"? Saint Ignatius said when you get this feeling you are in the presence of God.

TAKE HOME BAG

This week whenever you sit down to eat, use your imagination and pretend that Jesus is sitting at the table with you. Jesus is listening to the conversation. Jesus is laughing at the jokes. Jesus is stealing a French fry when you're not looking. Jesus is making that "slurpy" noise at the bottom of the cup. This is how Jesus wants you to think of him, as present and part of our lives every day.

TIP

The message of communion is this:
We're all in this together. Think about it.